A World of Intricacies

By
Anagha Ratish

© Anagha Ratish 2021

All rights reserved

All rights reserved by author. No part of this publication may be reproduced, stored in a retrieval system or transmitted in any form or by any means, electronic, mechanical, photocopying, recording or otherwise, without the prior permission of the author.

Although every precaution has been taken to verify the accuracy of the information contained herein, the author and publisher assume no responsibility for any errors or omissions. No liability is assumed for damages that may result from the use of information contained within.

First Published in July 2021

ISBN: 978-93-5472-029-1

BLUEROSE PUBLISHERS
www.bluerosepublishers.com
info@bluerosepublishers.com
+91 8882 898 898

Cover Design:
Priyanca

Typographic Design:
Namrata Saini

Distributed by: BlueRose, Amazon, Flipkart, Shopclues

To my grandparents, for never failing to be impressed with even the smallest of my achievements.

Acknowledgements

I have another long list of people to thank again, but I will try to keep it brief.

An enormous thank you to my entire family, (that includes my grandparents, uncles, aunts, cousins, great-uncles, great-aunts and all of my extended family) who have supported and encouraged me, throughout my journey.

A special thank you to my parents, for always believing in me.

Immense gratitude to all the reviewers, bookstagrammers and bloggers who have reviewed my earlier work. The feedback and support means a lot to me.

Lastly, and most importantly, thank you to all my readers for being willing to listen to the ramblings of an almost- teenage-girl and for helping me come this far.

Contents

Some Rather Philosophical Free-Verse Poetry, To Begin With

The Beginning

I must begin somewhere,
So, I don't see why I shouldn't,
Begin here,
As it is as good a place as any.

This is not,
Precisely a story,
But on the other hand,
Perhaps it is, of a sort.

Call it what you will,
This is the beginning of it,
Since I must begin,
Somewhere or the other.

A Tale of Good and Evil

This is not a tale of magic,
Or one of witchcraft.
Not a story of war and adventure,
But the battles around us.

A tale of good and evil,
But the evil are perhaps, the good.
Roles reversed, misunderstood,
Maybe the good are just afraid of change.

Words on paper are so simple to understand,
The good win, and the evil are defeated.
But are the evil as bad as you think?
Or are their intentions nobler than the good?

But our lives are stories too,
And everything is a peculiar shade of grey,
For the good are not always righteous,
And the evil sometimes are.

Perhaps this is, indeed, a tale of good and evil,
But it is for you to determine who is good and evil,
Who is black and who is white,
In this confusing world of grey.

The evil do great things,
More powerful than the good.
Why do you think that is?
Because black taints the white.

The Colour of the World

I have heard people say,
That the world is not black and white,
But what is the colour of the world then?
Besides a funny shade of grey.

The world is, nevertheless, presumed to be black
and white,
The good are snow-bright,
And the bad, charcoal.
But is the world a chessboard?

Maybe the world *is* just a funny shade of grey,
And we are flashes in the storm.
But nothing is ever black and white;
The world is not grey, but bright.

Every person is more than good,
More than evil;
They have hearts, souls,
Minds and thoughts.

I believe that the world is not black and white,
But not grey either.
The world explodes with colour,
That we just cannot see.

Change Will Come

Evil, or good, it is an ever-raging battle.
Never-ceasing, flashes of grey;
The good protect what is,
And the evil destroy and create anew.

But however long the good fight,
Change will come;
Fire will envelop the world,
And from ashes, a new world will emerge.

Perhaps the evil are not so selfish.
Perhaps it is the good who are slowly destroying
the world.
For change is eternal,
When nothing else is.

The evil are free, in a way the good can never
be;
They are content, with the knowledge that
change will come,
While the good are shackled with the hopes that
it will not.
Maybe it is the evil who are revolutionaries.

Either way, the evil will win,
For even the good are not always virtuous,
In the battle of what is right and what is good;
Of the meaning of justice, in the eyes of the law
and the heart.

But when smoke plumes through the world,
Of one thing, you can be certain;
Change will come, despite everything,
For change is the one thing that is permanent.

Belief

Is there such a thing as good and evil?
Is there really a black and white?
Or are the evil simply misunderstood,
Their intentions worthy to their own eyes?

Maybe there is no good and evil.
Maybe it's only a matter of belief,
Because everyone wants to hope,
But sometimes, hope is a curtain that obscures the
truth.

Everyone wants to believe,
That some are good and some are bad,
Because it is frightening to see,
That the monsters of this world are also people.

But living, breathing, thinking souls cannot be
labelled with a single word,
Be it good or evil.
Because there is always more to it,
Than what is above the surface.

We want to believe that good exists in the world;
Pure, whole-hearted good,
But there is a difference,
Between what is and what should be.

The Difference Between Right and Good

There is a difference between what is right and
what is good.
A difference between justice to the heart,
And justice to the law.
The law is vital, but not always right, or good.

The good make a choice, between what is right
and what is virtuous,
While the bad often choose the right;
Not in the eyes of the law,
But to their own heart.

What is right is the law,
What is good is from the heart;
But really, what is right?
For sometimes justice is right to the heart.

So, which path should you take?
When you stand at a crossroads,
To be good or to be righteous?
Justice or morality?

Hearts, and Other Flittish Things

I sometimes wonder,
Whether what the evil do,
Is justice to them,
If they listen to the whispers of the heart.

The evil are not so bad,
 If what they do is follow their hearts,
Which is what everyone,
Advises and ignores.

But often, we don't want to believe,
That the evil have hearts,
That they feel too,
That they are not so different from us.

Maybe that is why the scariest monsters are,
The most like us,
Because they remind us,
That we are the same, just working for different causes.

In that case, should you follow your heart,
If what you want is considered evil on the surface?
Should you follow your heart at all?
Because hearts are flittish things.

Noble, or Otherwise

Who are noble,
The good, who scramble to protect what is,
However awful it may be?
Or is it the bad who slowly build new worlds?

We know that there are problems,
In this enormous world,
But we only sit back,
And watch as our world crumbles.

There are those who fight for change,
Lawfully, and legally,
Slowly, harnessing change.
Are *they* evil?

Then there are those,
Who sacrifice everything,
To bring change,
Quick as lightning.

Which of them is braver?
When they fight for the same cause,
Evil, or not,
Noble, or otherwise.

Two Kinds of Evil

There are two types of evil,
If any.
One is the kind that changes the world,
And then there is a petty evil, spawned from
hostility.

Murder, perhaps is the latter,
While, say, destroying the world is the former.
The first is seldom found, in this world,
For the true revolutionaries are often labelled
insane.

Petty, or not, the murderer has reasons,
Although they do not always justify the act.
Unfortunately, evil is born from hate,
Which is often in unnecessary abundance, among
us humans.

Perhaps, if we had more of the kind of evil,
That changes the world,
The world would be,
A much better place.

Perhaps

Perhaps is a funny word.
It ignites a spark of hope,
Or a sense of dread,
A stronger word than others.

It's strange how the meaning changes;
The feelings change,
Depending on the way,
It is placed in a sentence.

Words are often,
More powerful than actions,
For they can destroy you with,
But a sound.

Words are powerful things,
Especially those that invoke hope.
Choose your words carefully,
For words are precious jewels.

Hope

Hope is a wonderful thing,
But dangerous,
For it takes but a second,
to shatter your dreams.

Hope is much like love,
Because you must open your heart.
To do either,
You must be vulnerable first.

But without hope,
What meaning does our world have?
Is there any worth to our lives,
When we cannot dream?

Hope is like a fire,
It blazes fiercely,
Until it burns out,
Leaving nothing but ashes.

Hope is a beautiful thing,
But terrible too,
For with hope, your heart can soar,
Before you come crashing down.

Although hope is often,
What gives us courage,
Seldom is it,
A good thing.

Hope makes us believe,
What we want to believe.
It obscures the real world,
In a shroud of smoke.

Hope is a two-faced creature,
It lifts you into the sky,
Only to find inky oblivion,
Waiting for you to pass.

Everyone hopes for happy endings,
Everyone wishes for good.
But rarely do these dreams come true,
After they warp our vision.

People say you can lie,
If it makes one happy;
But isn't that a kind of evil?
To make a heart rise, just to plummet further?

The wings of hope are glorious, yes
But fragile.
You may soar for one magnificent moment,
Before you hurtle into an abyss.

Problems and Solutions

I sometimes long,
To change the world;
To fix the bad parts,
And bring out the good.

But our world is so complicated,
 Burdened with laws, rules,
Moralities and feelings,
When life could be so simple.

But do we really want it to be?
If you could fix the world's problems,
With a snap of your fingers,
Would you want to?

Our lives could,
Someday, perhaps be simple,
But ask yourself,
Is simplicity really what you want?

Through the Window, from the Other Side

Everything in this world,
Is different from each perspective.
I sometimes wish if I could take a peek,
Through the window, from the other side.

What if the glass covering the window frame,
Is stained with vivid colours,
But we just can't see it,
And we are staring at only a blank sky.

Or maybe the glass is blank,
From the other side.
Maybe the ones on the other side,
Cannot see through.

Or perhaps both sides are blank,
And the people on both sides,
Are staring at nothing,
Except for a lucky few.

The fortunate are those who can see through,
the peepholes of even blank glass.
They are those who can dream,
even without hope.

A Chessboard World

If life really was black and white,
As people often remark,
Then life would be nothing but,
A complicated game of chess.

And where's the fun in that?
Although, some people,
Would find that enjoyable,
On the whole, I would rather not.

It would mean that things are,
Simple and straightforward,
While that is obviously,
Not true.

Life has no rules,
No one way,
To do things,
However simple.

For life is unpredictable,
Unexpected and bold,
And that is one thing,
We can forever count on.

Souls

Are souls real,
And does everyone have them?
I often wonder,
In my musings.

If souls were real,
And I had one,
What would it look like,
If it's supposed to be *me?*

Would it be wispy white?
The way it is in books.
Or would it be my favourite colour,
Or perhaps, a flower?

Perhaps souls do not exist at all,
And they are simply,
Manifestations of everything,
We want to believe.

That we, the good,
Have pure souls,
And the evil have corrupted souls;
That we are the light and they, the dark.

This World

There are so many,
Things in this complicated,
World that I wish to fix,
In an instant.

But I cannot,
For I am too young,
Too bold,
And supposedly too naive.

There are so many things,
I wish to fix,
But to do that,
I must go through them myself.

We preach about morals,
Hearts, souls and values,
But do we really mean it,
When it comes to reality?

When things are wrong,
I wonder why they can't be righted,
For it is a simple matter,
But there we go with opinions.

And so, I have learnt,
The world is not only about what is right or good,
But about power, influence,
Money, of course, and greed.

Curses

People say,
That it is a curse,
To be pretty, to be old,
To be clever.

But really,
It is a curse to *see*.
See all that is wrong,
In this vast world.

Some call it pessimism,
Others, realism,
Call it what you will,
It is still a curse.

It is the pessimists, realists,
Who are vital to the world,
For they see things as they are,
Without that shroud called hope.

Being realistic is not being pessimistic,
For the truth is what it is,
However you wish,
To sugar-coat it.

Like so many others,
This curse is,
Both a gift and a bane,
To see, when others cannot.

Humans

Humans are, sometimes,
The most despicable of all creatures,
Although I happen, to have,
The misfortune of being one myself.

This world is beautiful;
Every morning,
The azure sky is glazed with,
Cotton candy clouds.

At night,
The stars sprinkle the inky sky,
And the moon hangs steadily,
Like an ethereal lantern.

Clear water flows,
Down streams,
Emptying into the,
Salty, cerulean sea.

This world had everything we needed,
But no,
We sacrificed beauty,
Under the pretence of evolution.

Now the once-azure sky,
Is clouded,
Only by smoke,
and dust.

The stars are shrouded in,
Chemical fumes;
They shine as brightly as ever,
But we have masked their glow.

Contaminated water,
Drips slowly down streams,
Into the toxic,
once-cerulean sea,

After witnessing this,
Can you truly say,
That humans are the cleverest,
Of all the creatures on Earth?

Yes, the whole race is not responsible for this,
And yet,
We are to be blamed,
For the future.

Magic

Most believe,
That there is no such thing,
As magic,
But I think otherwise.

To us,
Everything we cannot,
Explain away with science,
Is magic.

We try to simplify everything,
With our mundane sciences,
For it would never do,
For things to simply *be*.

Science and magic,
Often go hand in hand.
For the things we have not discovered,
Are magic.

Other times, magic is,
Simply something,
Humans cannot wrap,
Their heads around.

So, truly, magic does exist
For magic,
Like most other things,
Is relative.

Power

What, truly, is power?
Is it money?
Or, perhaps, is it something deeper,
Something for which the heart yearns?

Everyone seeks power,
In some way,
Money is, of course, power,
But only in the most mundane sense.

Power is something that,
Everyone wants,
Deep inside,
But in different forms.

Everyone wants,
To be in control,
To have some restraint,
Over life.

So, everyone with power,
Is not corrupt,
For there are different kinds,
of power.

Love is a sort of power,
So is trust.
And a good mind,
Is more powerful than you think.

It is only the power,
Born from greed,
That corrupts,
The weak.

Righteousness

To do what is right,
Or what is good,
An eternal question,
That haunts me.

What is good,
 Is oft not right.
And that which is right,
Is seldom good.

But the ideas,
Of good and right,
Are warped,
In this world.

There are some things that should,
Be both good and right,
But seldom is it so,
In our lives.

Most believe that,
The law is right,
And our hearts are good,
But is it really so?

A Salve Called Time

Time, so oft a sweet salve,
That washes over all wounds,
Healing what nothing else can,
As it weaves together a broken heart.

When you suffer a loss,
You heart rips at the seams.
Time stitches and mends,
But loss leaves a scar.

Time is a kind of balsam,
But not always a remedy.
Time heals, yes,
But it can also hurt.

Grief can grow with time,
As can hate,
And bitterness feeds on you,
Till you cannot feel love.

Loss is a powerful thing.
I should dearly love to say,
That hope is more so,
But that would be, but a lie.

With the right herbs,
Salves *do* heal,
And wounds of loss
Can close.

Whether or not time stitches the wound,
Grief leaves a permanent scar,
That can never disappear,
Because loss is a cruel blade.

But time can make you forget,
So, pour yourself a chalice of years,
With just a dash of love,
And perhaps, you'll heal.

It is oft a bitter tale I tell,
And so is this.
Some wounds never heal,
But *that* is life.

Truth

Truth, that bitter potion,
That oft repels,
As the sweet scent of lies,
Draws victims.

To tell untruths, is simple.
The scent wafts invitingly,
Promising simplicity,
And a twisted joy.

The truth is, forsooth, bitter,
No one wants the truth.
They want to hear,
Only silken lies that suit their fancy.

Truth is a bitter elixir;
Lies are a sweet ensnare,
Deceptively sugared,
Laced with poison.

But lies tie an intricate web,
Eventually snarling you in.
However bitter truth may be,
Vincit omnia veritas.

Who Am I?

Who am I?
What defines me?
A collection of words,
Or a jumble of features and faces?

At the moment of writing this,
I have lived but twelve years,
And just eight coherent years.
Not a great deal of time, but enough.

At twelve, I am not taken very seriously,
Although I have published a book,
Pondered the world,
And gained the barest hint of wisdom.

Who am I?
Am I the person in my mind?
Or is the girl in others' minds,
More real, more *me*?

Who would you be,
If your face changed its shape,
And everything about you became just a bit
different?
Yourself, or someone else entirely?

I am not who I was a year ago,
And I was even more different two years ago.
Have I become someone else?
Or have I become more like *myself*?

Do these other versions of me,
Float around my person,
Like strangely familiar ghosts,
That haunt the depths of who I am?

Melancholy

There's a chill in the air.
There's a heaviness to my heart.
A deep melancholy,
Echoing, echoing.

A deep weariness resounds in my bones,
Dulling the world.
A restlessness pounds through me,
As if I am waiting for something.

But the world is bleached of colour;
The skies are grey.
The stale odour of melancholy,
Drifts and spreads.

The reason for this despondent state,
I know not,
But my soul weighs me down,
And my heart is made of stone.

The air is still;
There is no breeze,
To ruffle the grass and tousle the trees;
To carry this melancholy away.

And so, against the blank grey skies,
The melancholy hangs like a heavy cloud,
Stilling the breeze,
Of hope and contentment.

Dawn

A gentle breeze caresses treetops,
The crystal surface of a lake,
Ripples and stills,
As the sun appears on the horizon.

A rosy dawn,
With glistening dewdrops that,
Slide gingerly from green leaves,
And birds that twitter, high in the trees.

Soft streaks of colour,
Painting over the midnight canvas,
As the wind carries the night air,
Away, away.

Waiting

All our lives,
We wait for something,
One after the other,
For something to begin, and another to end.

The world always,
Holds its breath,
Anxious, restless,
Forever waiting.

It never ends,
This eternal anticipation,
For all of life,
Is a wait.

An Hourglass Called Time

Time is a strange thing,
Sometimes it slips through my fingers,
Like sand,
If sand scarred my hands.

Other times, it moves,
As if swimming against the current.
Slowly,
Each moment, eternity.

I often wish time would move faster,
But then I realize,
That a moment lasts only a second,
And when it is gone, it is gone forever.

But then, that is,
The hourglass called time.
Each grain of sand slipping away,
Until nothing is left.

Victory

Victory, defeat,
What is the difference,
If you learn,
Something new?

Is it a victory,
Only if you defeat another?
Or is victory,
Conquering oneself?

Is it really defeat,
If you best yourself,
Not another,
In a battle with your mind?

Destiny

Destiny, fate
Luck and fortune;
All concepts,
I do not entirely believe in.

Destiny,
Where divine threads of fate,
Are woven,
Into lives.

As though life is,
But a rather tragic book,
And invisible hands,
Turn pages unseen.

As though life,
Is a chessboard;
Each move planned,
And the next anticipated.

The Clock of Life

The clock of life,
Ticks,
And each day the clock,
Strikes twelve.

An endless circle,
Around and round,
The hands of time spin,
Ticking, ticking.

Until one day,
The clock stops ticking,
The hands freeze in place,
And the chime does not resound again.

The ticking sinks,
Into a memory;
The tinkling chime,
But an echo.

Lies

Often, we see the world,
Through a lens of lies,
The truth a dark reality.
That most do not wish to see.

We obscure our views,
With the glaze of hope,
The veil of lies,
The curtain of dreams.

A lie,
Warps the truth;
Call it what you may,
A white lie, a dream, a hope.

Truth, however bitter,
Is a tonic to see the world as it is,
While lies churn into a sugary poison,
Dimming your vision.

Façades

Everyone wears a mask,
Of some sort;
Some kind of façade,
Intentional or not.

For some it is the veil,
Of concealed deception.
For others, the shield of being what one is not,
And hoping it becomes reality.

But not all façades,
 Are cunningly created;
Some are only shields,
To protect oneself.

Reality

Reality, a harsh dimension,
Not many wish to see.
Reality, a place where the view,
Is not rose-tinted.

Reality, where hope exists only,
To keep you going,
Till you fall harder,
Than ever before.

Reality, where time is slow,
Then slipping fast,
Until your precious moments,
Have all crept away.

Reality, a place where,
The sun shines into your eyes.
Reality, a world where the winds,
Blow through you.

Reality, a region that is scalding, one moment,
And glacial the next;
Rarely perfect,
Rarely just right.

Happiness

What is the secret,
To happiness, in truth?
Money, perhaps?
Or maybe love?

But even those laden,
with gold baubles,
and diamond trinkets,
Are not always happy.

On the other hand,
Love doesn't pay the bills,
Or put food on the table,
And you cannot starve to death happily.

The truth is,
The meaning of happiness changes.
Sometimes it only means,
That you are not *un*happy.

The Ending

I began at the beginning,
So, this requires a suitable end,
For all things end,
Happy or not.

This is not a happy ending,
Nor a sad one;
This is merely,
An ending.

Not all stories end with a happy event,
Neither do they all end with death.
So, let us just say,
That it is simply an ending.

A Collection of Haikus, About a Variety of Things

Haiku #1

With a cup of tea,
I curl up on the warm couch,
A book in my hands.

Haiku #2

The sun shines brightly,
In the vivid azure sky,
Clouds of cotton drift.

Haiku #3

The words bubble up,
I write, but not fast enough,
Weaving a story.

Haiku #4

The clock ticks slowly,
I tap my foot, impatient,
But time seems to stop.

Haiku #5

I hum and listen,
To the melodies that ring,
Only in my head.

Haiku #6

The heat visible,
Shimmering in the blue sky,
The world looks wilted.

Haiku #7

The night air is cool,
The sky is a midnight curtain,
Obscuring the world.

Haiku #8

Hope is a curtain,
Obscuring reality,
Obscuring the truth.

Haiku #9

The world is mundane,
Filled with ordinary, so,
Paint it with magic.

Haiku #10

The clouds loom heavy,
In the fast darkening sky,
It will rain today.

Haiku #11

Staring at my pen,
I search for new ideas,
Grasping one, I write.

Haiku #12

The candle of life,
Is, but a flickering one,
Unsteady, shaking.

Haiku #13

Hope is just over,
The horizon, so close yet,
Forever unreached.

Haiku #14

The world holds its breath,
The azure sky is cloudless,
Waiting for something.

Haiku #15

Time, oft a salve,
Time, which slips through my fingers,
Like the sand of life.

And to End,
An Extra from
Celestia Chronicles
(My First Book)

The world was slowly dissolving into chaos,
When a zaralia stumbled in.
But not this world,
A world with magic that would make your head
spin.

Celestia- a world of pixies,
With four kingdoms that flourished;
Sprawling forests, shimmering lakes,
And rulers who were cherished.

The wane began when the great king of
Emberglass,
The kingdom of Infernos in the north,
Was murdered with his wife and eldest daughter,
alas,
Leaving young princess Zyra to rule forth.

No sooner had the queen ascended her throne,
That she dropped her sweet facade,
She killed, looted and pillaged,
And burnt down the cities that were in her eyes,
deeply flawed.

What happened next is unclear,
For the kingdom was shrouded in magic and mist.
The people could not rebel for fear,
That the queen would hunt them if they resist.

So, two sisters, Sapphire and Willow Windsley,
Decided to re-establish Crystalhaven,
A council founded by Queen Sereia,
Decades ago to steady the shaken.

Sereia was a good queen,
But slightly bizarre;
The mysterious twinkle in her eyes could
prominently be seen,
And her love for riddles was known throughout
the kingdom, far.

She was a naiad, queen of Careldon,
Queen of all the nymphs,
A long time ago, an age far gone,
when she split the kingdom into two.

Careldon and Delyra,
They were called,
Delyra for the dryads and Careldon for the naiads,
The kingdoms were appalled.

But Queen Sereia remained on the throne,
Until she passed it on to her heirs;
A dryad and a naiad,
And passed on her worries and cares.

And then she disappeared,

On a silent silver night,
Gone, not far, nor near
She simply vanished, out of sight.

Decades later, a zaralia tripped through the
worlds,
To Delyra, to a secret valley, to a secret sanctuary;
The home of Sapphire Windsley,
Who was elusive as a faerie.

The zaralia's name was Adaire Quicksilver,
And Sapphire was astonished to see,
The zaralia that they had been waiting for,
The one who would harness the power of the sea.

She was taken to Crystalhaven,
Battling to free Emberglass;
From the reign of the queen with hair of raven;
And Adaire met Faye, another naiad, with eyes
the colour of grass.

Through adventures, out of battles, and into
mysteries,
Adaire stumbled past,
Until she found the missing queen,
Queen Sereia, at last.

A secret kingdom, Aquioa,

Created by the queen,
With the magic of the water and the sea,
In every blade of grass, there was much beauty to
be seen.

Queen Sereia now looked even stranger,
With turquoise hair and deep blue skin;
She directed them to Rivertide,
Her dagger, famous for harnessing the power of
the water within.

They retrieved the long-lost dagger from the
dwarves,
Who were the thieves,
The dwarves were perhaps as strange as the
queen,
With skin the colour of mud and clay, and clothes
woven of leaves.

Through treachery and peril,
They escaped through secret paths,
And returned the essential dagger to the queen,
Who seemed to be relieved to have avoided any
blood baths.

What happens next must be seen,
Can Adaire, Sapphire and Faye,
Defeat the evil queen,
And keep evil at bay?

www.ingramcontent.com/pod-product-compliance
Lightning Source LLC
Chambersburg PA
CBHW021336160726
47994CB00007B/2724